No Fair!

William Chin
Illustrated by Doreen Gay-Kassel

HOUGHTON MIFFLIN HARCOURT

www.Rigby.com
800-531-5015

Contents

Good News That's Bad News

Everything had been going so well until Mother told Yun the good news that actually turned out to be bad news.

Yun had begun swimming earlier in the year because her soccer coach thought it would be good for strengthening her legs. Yun soon discovered that she was good at swimming and she loved it, and this pleased her soccer coach.

The coach was not so pleased when Yun told her that she had joined the pool's junior relay swimming team, but Ms. Serrano responded to the announcement calmly, with a shrug and a smile. Yun would still be on the soccer team, but she would have to miss a few practices. She felt a little sorry that she had to disappoint her soccer coach, but mostly she was glad to be on the swim team because it was so much fun!

Besides, she'd met Lum, a ten-year-old girl on the team who was tall, smart, and funny. They weren't in the same grade, but Lum went to the same Chinese school that Yun and her sister Jen attended on Saturdays. When Jen first joined the relay team, Lum had given her many swimming tips, and the two girls always seemed to be talking and laughing together while they waited their turn to go into the water. Before long Mother started giving Lum a ride home after practice, and now the two girls had become great friends.

One day at swim practice, their coach announced that the junior relay team was going to the Valley Hill Regional Swim Meet in three weeks! "You've all worked hard, and I think you have a good chance in the relay race, so please check with your parents to see if you can go." Once they found out that everyone was able to go, the team spent the next few weeks working harder than they ever had before.

So here it was, Tuesday of the week of the swim meet. Yun's father was very disappointed that he had to be out of town for a business meeting, but Yun thought that she could depend on Mother to take her and Lum to Valley Hill.

But now, unexpectedly, Mother had to go out of town to help Auntie May, who had recently adopted a baby. The baby was arriving sooner than planned—and Mother was the only family member who could take the time to help Auntie May with the new baby.

Yun was upset. Who was going to take her to Valley Hill? And she knew that Lum's family didn't even own a car, so how was Lum going to get there?

Yun suddenly remembered the first time she had dived into the pool and landed flat on her stomach—ouch! That was just how she felt now. No fair!

2
Grandparents in Charge

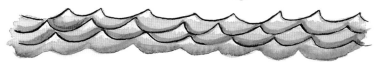

That night Yun stood in Mother's bedroom and pleaded, "You can't leave—not *this* weekend!"

"Yun, I've told you already that I need to be at Auntie May's home by tomorrow because Uncle Seng has to be at work during the day, even on Saturday, and there's no one else to help your aunt right now," Mother said as she continued packing her bag for the trip.

"I don't care!" cried Yun. Instantly she was sorry, and only partly because Mother stopped folding her blouse and gave her a stern look.

Yun knew that it was a mean thing to say, and in fact she really liked Auntie May a lot, and she really did care. At any other time, the news about the baby would be thrilling, but right now the only thing Yun could say was, "I didn't really mean I don't care, Mother, but there's just no other way for Lum and me to get to Valley Hill!"

"I've asked your grandmother to be in charge of taking you and Lum to the meet," said Mother, "and I've given her complete instructions on how to get there. You'll have to take the bus and then the train, but trust me, it will work out just fine, so please stop worrying and let me finish packing."

Yun thought about Grandmother taking them all the way to Valley Hill on public transportation. Would Grandmother be able to do this? Yun left her mother's room, but she still wasn't sure about these plans.

Jen had been standing outside her mother's room. She had been thinking about going in, but when she heard her mother's tone of voice and saw a very unhappy Yun leave so quickly, she bit her lip and stayed outside.

Jen didn't have to worry about a swim meet, but she wasn't too happy about Mother leaving, either. Mother had arranged for Grandfather to pick her up after school for the next few days.

If someone had asked Jen whether she or her sister was better at taking bad news, she would have to admit that big sister Yun was the one who usually stayed calm. It was no big surprise, then, that Jen responded with what could have been described as pure panic when Mother had told her that Grandfather would be the one picking her up.

"It will be OK, Jen. It's only for a few days, not even a whole week!" Mother had explained over and over, but Jen was not convinced.

Grandfather didn't dress like her friends' moms and dads. When he came home from the bakery, he sometimes still had his apron on—what would her friends think? Would they make fun of her? No fair!

Yun went to the kitchen, where Grandmother was sitting at the table with a book and some magazines spread out in front of her. Three times a week, she helped Grandmother with her English. Tonight Yun thought that she'd better make sure Grandmother was up to the challenge of getting her to Valley Hill.

Yun stood next to the table, her hands on her hips, and asked, "Grandmother, have you ever taken the bus farther than the bookstore, and do you know how the trains work? Do you know how much things cost and when you need to have the exact change?"

"Slow down, young lady, and show a little respect! Shouldn't you already know these things about your own grandmother? Of course I know how to get around, and besides," she said with a twinkle in her eye, "I'll have you along to help me!"

The Trouble with Grown-ups

The next morning, Grandfather walked Jen to school, taking her down unusual streets and through the park. "It's more peaceful, and the scenery is better," he explained, and this suited Jen just fine, since it also meant that they probably wouldn't run into any of her friends. She walked along quietly, while Grandfather marched down the street like a tour guide, looking all around and pointing out birds and plants that he recognized.

They were about a block away from the school when Jen tugged on Grandfather's hand, stopping at a corner in front of a white house with tall bushes in front.

"OK, Grandfather," said Jen, "this is where I get picked up after school."

Of course, this wasn't quite right. Mother usually waited for her right in front of the school, but Jen didn't want Grandfather to know this. She looked at him steadily, hoping that he wouldn't ask her any questions.

Grandfather did have a strange look on his face, not exactly a frown and not exactly a smile. He stood there for a moment, looking up and down the street, but finally he nodded to her and said, "OK, Jen, I will be waiting for you right here this afternoon after school."

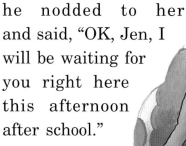

17

Relieved, Jen turned quickly and began walking the rest of the way to school by herself. Maybe nobody would see Grandfather with her while Mother was gone.

Lum was on her way to school, too, and while she walked, she thought about what her parents had told her last night—that swimming was taking a lot of her time.

They had a very long discussion about it while they ate dinner at the big table in the kitchen of her parents' restaurant. Lum helped out there after school, that is, except on the days when she went to the pool to practice her swimming. Her parents explained that things were busy at the restaurant, and they wished she could spend more time helping them.

If only they could see her swimming, Lum thought, maybe they'd feel differently about it, but they were always at the restaurant. Lum sighed, thinking that her parents would probably never see her swim. No fair!

Behind the Scenes

That afternoon, Jen dashed out of her classroom as quickly as possible, without stopping to talk to any of her friends. "I have to hurry and meet Grandfather," she thought, "so that he doesn't have a chance to walk all the way to the school!" She walked quickly past teachers, weaving back and forth between the other kids, and out the door.

Jen ran down the sidewalk, relieved that Grandfather wasn't in front of the school, but wondering why she didn't even see him at the corner. She ran to the white house, stopping breathlessly in front of the tall bushes where, just around the corner and out of sight, stood Grandfather.

"Well there you are!" he said, smiling broadly. "Shall we go?" He had been standing there reading a book, but now he tucked it under his arm.

After they had walked in silence for a while, Grandfather cleared his throat and said, "Jen, wouldn't you like me to meet you right in front of the school?"

Jen, too nervous to look at him, said, "Oh . . . well . . . sure . . . I guess that might be a good thing to do sometime, Grandfather."

"Tell me, do you think that I look funny compared to your friends' parents?"

"It's true," thought Jen, "Grandfather really *can* read minds, just like Mother and Father really *do* have eyes in the back of their heads!"

Jen didn't say anything, which was almost the same as telling Grandfather that he was absolutely right. She tried not to look at Grandfather because she didn't want him to read her mind again!

Most days Yun would have walked home with Jen, but today she and Lum were walking together, laughing and talking. Yun had permission to visit with Lum at the restaurant that her parents owned, and she was looking forward to it. As they walked, Yun told Lum about last night's English lesson at home, describing the questions she had asked Grandmother about getting around on the bus and the train. Yun admitted that she had even made Grandmother practice all the words she thought she would need on Saturday.

"It's going to be such a bother, dragging around our bags and switching to the train and worrying about Grandmother, too," complained Yun.

"I think your grandmother will be OK," Lum said laughing.

"Well, maybe so, but I'm still a little upset about my mother going off to stay with Auntie May this weekend. How could such a little baby turn out to be such big trouble?"

Lum's parents' restaurant had a big window with a neon sign that read CHINESE FOOD—TAKE OUT. A small bell rang as Lum and Yun opened the door and stepped into the small waiting area with its red plastic couch and two red chairs. The only table in the room was a small round one with a big potted plant on it.

"Mom, I'm here, and Yun is with me!" called Lum as they walked around the end of the counter. The girls went through a swinging door and into a space with a large table and some chairs nearby. Beyond that was the kitchen, where Lum's parents were standing.

Lum's mother and father were both wearing white aprons. Mrs. Eng was a short, round woman, while Mr. Eng was taller and quite thin. They politely greeted Yun in Chinese and offered the girls juice and almond cookies for a snack.

Lum's mother told them both to do their homework, which they did at the big table that served both as a work place and as a dining table when the family sat down for meals.

Yun had never been behind the counter of a restaurant, so she kept stealing glances at all the interesting things that Lum's parents were doing in the kitchen.

It was almost dinnertime, so Lum had to start work, too, helping her parents by writing down the orders from customers who called or came in. Yun was impressed that Lum had so much responsibility, and she also learned that because Mr. and Mrs. Eng didn't speak English very well, they let Lum do most of the talking with customers.

Later Grandmother came to pick up Yun, and she seemed to get along quite well with Lum's mother. The two of them chattered away in Chinese for a while as Yun gathered up her things. On the way home, Yun asked Grandmother if she had to speak English at work.

"Not very much, Yun," she said, "because most of the customers at the bookstore speak Chinese."

It was then that Yun finally figured out why Grandmother liked to practice English with her—she didn't have many other opportunities to practice!

What a Surprise!

The next day at school, Yun's thoughts were not on her schoolwork. Her friends could tell that she wasn't paying attention, and Mr. Etienne had to ask her a question twice before she heard him. Berto leaned over and whispered, "Earth to Yun! What's the matter with you?"

"This evening will be our last practice before the swim meet, and I'm nervous about a lot of things," she explained to Berto.

Yun jumped up and dashed out of the room the minute the bell rang. The school hallway was a zoo, as it nearly always was at the end of the day.

She wound her way through the halls and finally found Jen, who obviously had been looking for her and seemed a little frantic. Jen grabbed her hand, pulling Yun and rushing her out the door.

"We have to meet Grandfather down the street and around the corner!" she exclaimed, dragging her big sister behind her.

They were nearly there when Grandfather came walking around the corner toward them, and what a surprise! He was wearing a new navy blue suit, and he looked so businesslike that they hardly recognized him.

"Well, ladies, how do I look?"

Jen had felt funny about how Grandfather dressed before, but somehow this made her even more embarrassed, and she looked around to make sure no one she knew had spotted them. Suddenly speechless, she grabbed his hand and steered him around the corner toward home.

"Hey, what's going on here?" Yun asked. Yun hadn't known that Grandfather even owned such a suit, and the sight of him in it had stunned her.

"Oh, it's nothing, really," Grandfather laughed, "except that Jen thought I looked too different from her friends' parents, so I thought I'd wear something special for her today."

"Jen, you'd better stop acting so silly!" scolded Yun. "You didn't really make Grandfather wear fancy clothes to meet you, did you? And did you tell him that he wasn't supposed to wait for you in front of the school? You know that isn't right!"

Jen's silence only made Yun angrier—but she had to admit that Grandfather did look pretty good in that suit!

Later that afternoon, Yun and Grandmother talked about Jen as they were on their way to her team's practice at the pool. "Don't be too hard on Jen," said Grandmother. "It isn't always easy to feel like you belong, and Jen has a harder time of it than you ever did."

"So where in the world did Grandfather get that beautiful suit?"

"Your Grandfather is full of surprises, isn't he?" laughed Grandmother.

Soon they arrived at the pool for the team practice. It was great to see Yun's swimming buddies—Myra, Armando, and, of course, Lum.

Yun changed into her swimsuit and then went up into the stands to give Grandmother her school English book—"I thought you might get bored and want to practice," she said with a warm smile.

Their coach made them work hard during their warm-up, but everyone on the team enjoyed this time in the water because the coach made it fun, and it also prepared them for their relay practice.

Armando was first, and he crouched at the end of the pool with his toes curled over the edge. The coach blew her whistle, and Armando dove into the water. The members of the relay team dove in, one after the other, with an ease that they hadn't felt even one month ago.

Yun was so pleased with the way she was able to glide through the water during her laps that she happily shouted, "I'm a fish!" as she popped out of the pool.

The team members spent the next half hour working to improve one move or another, and by the time they were done, they all felt ready for Saturday's meet. But even when the coach gave them some last-minute reminders and told them they looked great, Yun was still nervous because this was her first swim meet ever!

As they left the pool, Lum and Yun were talking excitedly about the swim meet when Grandmother interrupted by asking, "Lum, are your parents going to come to watch you?"

Lum was quiet, hesitating for just a moment before answering, "No, Mrs. Moy, it's always very busy at the restaurant, so they have to stay there. Maybe they'll come to see me another time."

Yun began chatting again, but Grandmother saw that Lum was suddenly quiet. Grandmother took out a pen and found a piece of blank paper tucked between two pages of Yun's English book.

"Lum, may I please have your phone number so I can talk to your mother and make sure that I understand the plans for meeting you on Saturday?"

As Grandmother wrote down the phone number, she smiled to herself. Perhaps in her own way she'd turn out to be as full of surprises as Grandfather!

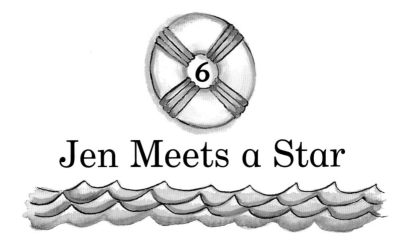

Jen Meets a Star

It was the end of the school day on Friday, and Jen stood on the front steps of the school, waiting impatiently for Yun—where could she be? Jen's friends were all around, but Yun wasn't anywhere to be seen, though Jen was sure that Yun had told her to wait here.

When Yun finally appeared, Jen urged, "Let's go, let's go!" Grabbing Yun's hand, she turned and started down the steps. As she did, she saw . . . Grandfather, right in front of the school, and looking his usual self in his baggy pants, his work shirt, and his worn shoes! Jen froze, pulling Yun to a sudden stop, not knowing what to do or where to go.

To her surprise, several of her classmates called out to Grandfather as if they knew him.

"Hey, look, it's Mr. *Bao!*"

"Mr. *Bao,* Mr. *Bao!*"

"Wow, what are you doing at our school?"

By now, Grandfather was so surrounded by Jen's classmates that his astounded grandchildren couldn't get near him. After returning the greetings, he called out to Jen and Yun, "Hello, girls, ready to go home?"

The questions from Jen's friends came so fast that she couldn't think.

"Do you know Mr. *Bao,* too?"

"Are you related to him?"

"That's not Mr. *Bao.* That's my grandfather," insisted Jen, a little confused by all the strange questions.

"Doesn't he work at the Chinese bakery?" asked her friend Jamila. "A lot of us like to go there and get those yummy steamed buns—*bao*—for a snack, but we never knew that Mr. *Bao* was your grandfather!" Jen's friends were impressed!

"Wow, he's your grandfather?"

"I'll bet you get to eat *bao* all the time."

All of a sudden, Grandfather seemed like a rock star.

Later as they walked home, Jen thought it over very carefully and finally decided that she would stop being embarrassed about her grandfather. She wondered, though, why Grandfather kept smiling.

Over dinner Jen chattered on about her "famous" Grandfather as Grandmother and Yun listened in amusement. Then Yun asked Grandmother if she was all ready for tomorrow morning, and Grandmother assured her that everything was set. Not only that, but Yun would have her own cheering section, because Jen was coming along, and Grandfather had rearranged his bakery schedule so that he could join them, too.

"Yun will have the famous Mr. *Bao* cheering for her!" announced Jen, and that made them all laugh.

A Great Day!

Saturday morning started clear and bright, so quiet and still that even the birds must have been sleeping in. Lum waited at the bus stop and looked down the empty street. There was still no sign of the bus coming.

A tiny speck appeared in the distance and soon grew into the shape of a bus. It pulled up to the curb, and Lum saw Yun waving from a window.

Lum boarded the bus and saw that Yun's whole family had come along. Why couldn't her parents be more like Yun's family?

"Hi, everybody," said Lum, grasping her bag tightly as she made her way down the aisle of the bus and sat down next to Yun. She talked with Yun as Jen kept interrupting the two older girls, trying to get their attention. Grandfather and

Grandmother sat across the aisle and talked softly to each other.

Grandmother knew exactly how to get to Valley Hill. After getting off the bus, they boarded a train, and after what seemed like forever, they finally arrived at the train station near Valley Hill pool.

Lum and Yun greeted their teammates, then listened as the coach instructed them to begin their stretches and warm-ups. The Moy family wished them luck and went to find a good seat in the stands.

Yun usually found stretches boring, but she was glad to do them today because she was still a little nervous and they kept her mind off the upcoming race. Now it was time to get into the water for their warm-up laps.

As Yun entered the pool, she looked around to find her family in the stands and waved to them. Then she stopped, stared, and swam over to Lum. "Hey, isn't that your mother sitting right next to my grandmother?"

Lum looked, and her heart leaped, because it really was her mom. At that moment, she saw Yun's grandmother say something and nod in Lum's direction. Lum's mother looked at her and waved.

A voice over the speakers interrupted, "Swimmers, the meet is about to begin. Please end your warm-ups."

The team relay race was about to begin, and though Lum had been very nervous before, her stomach was churning now, because for the first time ever, her mother would be watching her swim!

The announcer called their team's name, and they took their positions in their lane. The starting swimmers got into position, the buzzer sounded, and the swimmers leaped forward as the crowd roared.

When Armando returned and touched the side of the pool, Yun jumped in, swam to the other side, turned around, and swam back. Next it was Myra's turn, and then Lum, the team's strongest swimmer, swam the last lap of the relay. Lum glided, her fingers touched the side, and it was over!

Everyone on the team was chattering excitedly—everyone except Lum, who scanned the crowd for a familiar face. There . . . yes, there were the Moys, and with them was her mom smiling proudly.

Lum scarcely heard the Moys telling her and Yun how well their team had done, because she and her mother were too busy smiling at each other. Finally her mother said, "Very good, Lum! Next time maybe your father can watch you swim."

Lum smiled. She was so happy that her mom had come to see her swim, and she was even happier that her mom thought that there should be a next time. What a great day this was!

Home Again

As if the day had not already been exciting enough, Mother came home a whole day early. "Who wants to see pictures of the new baby?" Mother asked as she put her bags down. Yun and Jen rushed to greet her, and Grandmother and Grandfather joined them as they gathered around Mother and the photos that she had brought home.

"It's a boy, and he is very healthy and very beautiful!" said Mother. "Everything went just fine, and Auntie Ying is there now to help Auntie May."

Mother turned to Yun and asked how things went at Valley Hill. Though Yun was still just a little disappointed that her mother hadn't been there to see the swim meet, she smiled as she showed her medal to Mother and proudly announced that her team had won third place, which her coach had said was excellent for a junior team's first time in the regional meet.

"So how did Grandmother do in getting you there?"

"She did great," said Yun, "and do you know what else she did? Grandmother was very sneaky and called Lum's mother Friday night and persuaded her to take time off from work to come see Lum swim."

Grandmother looked both very proud of herself and slightly hurt. "Yun, there was nothing sneaky about it! Don't you agree that everyone wants to share special times with special people?" Yun nodded and grinned at Grandmother.

"And Jen," said Mother, turning to her younger daughter, "how did things go for you?"

"Mother," said Jen with a look of wide-eyed wonder, "did you know that Grandfather is . . . *famous?*"